INDIE AUTHOR MAGAZINE

HELLO AND WELCOME!

I'm Indie Annie, and I'm thrilled you're reading this gorgeous full-color version of IAM. Did you know that you can also access all the information, education, and inspiration in our app? It's available on both the iOS App Store and Google Play. And for those that prefer to listen to me read articles, you can pop over to Spotify or our website. Happy Reading!

X

IndieAuthorMagazine.com

TRANSLATIONS

22

IS YOUR BOOK MULTILINGUAL?

Considerations for the Translation Question

28

THERE'S NO "I" IN TRANSLATE

What's it Take to Find Your Dream Translation Team?

34

MARKETING TRANSLATIONS

ON THE COVER

PUBLISHER
Chelle Honiker

CREATIVE DIRECTOR
Alice Briggs

CONSULTING EDITOR
Nicole Schroeder

COPY EDITOR
Lisa Thompson

WRITERS
Angela Archer
Elaine Bateman
Patricia Carr
Laurel Decher
Fatima Fayez
Gill Fernley
Greg Fishbone
Remy Flagg
Chrishaun Keller Hanna
Jac Harmon

WRITERS
Marion Hermannsen
Kasia Lasinska
Bre Lockhart
Anne Lown
Sìne Màiri MacDougall
Merri Maywether
Lasairiona McMaster
Susan Odev
Nicole Schroeder
Emilia Zeeland

PUBLISHER
Athenia Creative
6820 Apus Dr.
Sparks, NV, 89436 USA
775.298.1925

ISSN 2768-7880 (online)–ISSN 2768-7872 (print)

From the Publisher

WHEN YOU'RE JUST A LITTLE STITIOUS

Like Michael Scott from *The Office*, I'm not superstitious, but I am a *little* "stitious." I don't open umbrellas inside. I throw spilled salt over my left shoulder. I don't walk under ladders.

And I never say, "It's going to be a calm week."

Because that's when you know it will most definitely *not* be a calm week.

As a startup, most weeks we buckle up and hold on and try to catch this tiger by the tail. There's a lot we do that mirrors what indie authors do, like keeping up with social media posts, running ads, writing the next release, and making sure our newsletter goes out.

I had a moment last week when it seemed too calm. Too quiet. Too peaceful.

It made me nervous.

I ran through the project lists, obsessively checking missed tasks or things I must have forgotten. I sent frantic Slack messages asking for status reports.

Nothing was on fire. Nothing broken. I hadn't missed a major milestone.

It wasn't calm before the storm. It was just calm.

We finally hit the stride the entire team had worked toward for the last nine months since we launched. The processes we'd implemented and the amazing people we'd hired were performing brilliantly.

I relaxed a little.

And then I knocked on wood.

To Your Success,
Chelle

Chelle Honiker, Publisher
Indie Author Magazine

LastPass •••|®

KEEP YOUR PASSWORD SAFE

Auto-pilot for all your passwords

Writelink.to/lastpass

Dear Indie Annie,

My family thinks I'm wasting my time writing. They interrupt me frequently and expect me to drop what I'm doing since they don't think I'm doing anything important. How can I convince them I want this to be a career, not a hobby?

Frustrated with Family in Flagstaff

DEAR FRUSTRATED,

Oh my lovely, I feel your pain as will most of your fellow writers reading about your plight.

Many of us will have faced similar challenges. Personally, I found my boss at my old day job most unsupportive of my writing while on company time. She would constantly ask me to do the tasks I was being paid to do and was most impolite.

I mean, seriously, one would think she paid me out of her own pocket.

But I digress. You, my dear, are not talking about stealing a few minutes away from your unenlightened employer. You are talking about your family: loved ones whose approval is important and whose support you naturally crave. As a result, their rejection of your dreams and ambitions can bite much deeper. They can also be clingy, needy time-sucks that drain every molecule of energy from your being. Or perhaps, that's only my children.

My boss may berate me, but my children's disapproval wounds my soul. Don't they realize I'm doing this for them? This is not like Jim-Bob's stamp collection or Aunt Mabel's quilt of the best serial killers from *Criminal Minds* season eight. This is work—really hard work. Amazing, fulfilling, creative work but also an actual professional occupation I want to carve a career in.

Why don't they understand?

Because society, media, books, and films have conditioned us to believe that writers are a gifted elite who retreat to log cabins, working in isolation to meet the demands of a pushy publishing house or literary agent. These mythical beasts receive enormous advances they then need to honor. They have obligations to the big man, and therefore, we must respect their "do not disturb" signs. They are also loners, outcasts who live like hermits away from the daily expectations of family and friends, emerging only to go on glamorous book tours and appear on *Oprah*.

If you are desperately

Need help from your favorite Indie Aunt?
Ask Dear Indie Annie a question at
IndieAnnie@indieauthormagazine.com

snatching opportunities to write during your normal day in between your job and other responsibilities, then they think you aren't a real writer. At least not like the ones on TV, right? Therefore, your cute pastime is merely a hobby. Perhaps you make some money from your sweet little endeavors, but then Aunt Mabel sold a few quilts on Etsy. How is your hobby any different?

My advice to you is two-fold: Build bridges or build walls. Let's start with bridges, as they're much easier. Take some time to show your family and friends what you want to achieve. Explain to them how indie publishing works; maybe even leave a few print copies of this fair publication on the coffee table or in the throne room.

Explain to them how other writers can give up the day job; perhaps even introduce them to those authors, particularly in your genre or, better yet, someone they have read themselves who is making a living through indie publishing. If you aren't sure, simply check out some of the six- or seven-figure authors we feature here every month.

If that fails or if they respond in disbelief with "Well, that's all very nice for them, dear, but ... " then you need to put up some boundaries or walls. Did I mention my children were "clingy, needy time-sucks?" I didn't mean it, of course. I love them deeply and would do anything to make them happy. But I must also attend to my own needs. As a writer, one of those specific needs is time to write.

Now, many authors are skilled at grabbing productive writing sprints wherever they find themselves alone or underoccupied. (I mentioned sneaking in some words during the day job.) And such creativity can work wonders for your productivity. Most, though, need dedicated, uninterrupted time to put their head down and focus.

If this is you and you are still disrupted, even after explaining why you want to be left alone, get tough and build that wall. Anticipate others' needs in advance and prepack their lunches or snacks; arrange for someone else to carpool; and hire a babysitter, dog sitter, or even a husband sitter if required. Go somewhere else to work, such as a cafe or park. Then turn off all outside interference, just as if you were in an important meeting with the President, Her Majesty The Queen, or Beyoncé.

This time is sacred. Treat it as such.

Put that meeting in your diary/calendar or in the family organizer in the kitchen, and then throw up an impenetrable force field. You don't go out, and you let nothing in.

When you are a successful author, those around will finally understand you have a deadline to meet for your pushy publisher, which in this case is you. ∎

Happy Writing,
Indie Annie

10 TIPS FOR
BOOKBUB

No doubt you're reading this, hoping we'll divulge the ultimate secret to getting accepted for a BookBub Featured Deal. And of course, we're going to talk about it. But there's far more to BookBub than just that.

1 SNAG A BOOKBUB FEATURED DEAL

Well, we have to start with this one. Sadly, we can't guarantee you a featured deal—we wish! But at least we can give you a few tips that may improve your chances.

A BookBub Featured Deal is the great white whale. BookBub has an enormous audience, and getting a featured deal could rocket your book, and quite possibly your career, to the next level. You could sell thousands of books and reach readers you couldn't possibly have reached so quickly on your own. Seriously, if you can afford to do it—it is quite spendy—start applying.

Before you fill in the form for a deal, make sure your book is as appealing as possible with a great genre-focused cover, a polished blurb, and as many reviews as you can get your hands on. You'll also need to either make your book free or offer a hefty discount. It's not unheard of for people to get a featured deal when they're in Kindle Unlimited, but BookBub wants to show off its recommendations to as many people as possible, so wide books do seem to have a better chance.

Then, it's a case of flexibility and extreme persistence. You might get a deal on your first go, or you might still be trying after submitting every month for years, but don't give up!

② BLING UP YOUR PROFILE

Before we move on to the other types of alerts on BookBub, one thing that can help you get attention is to claim your author profile and fill it in fully, along with adding your books. You'll get some free features straightaway, including the possibility of appearing in the suggested authors list for new signups who read your genre and in the recommended author emails that BookBub sends out.

You can add your books to BookBub's database, and readers will be able to bookmark them and add a deal alert in case you run a discount or a freebie offer. Your bio and image will appear on each of your book pages, with a "Follow" button to encourage readers to sign up for your alerts, and on BookBub's Discover Authors page (https://bookbub.com/discover-aiuthors).

③ APPLY FOR "NEW RELEASES FOR LESS" ALERTS

This alert is different from a featured deal as your e-book doesn't have to be discounted to qualify, so if you get accepted, you could make quite a nice sum with this one. BookBub will accept a range of different book types as long as it is a fiction book over 150 pages or a nonfiction book over 100 pages. For this alert, you need to apply like you would for a featured deal, and BookBub will select the books they feel are suitable. You can start applying six months before your book is due out, but this is another paid feature, so you will need a budget. What do they want to hear? According to BookBub's website, "In order to help our editors know whether your new book might be a good fit for our readers, we'd recommend including links to early reviews from bloggers or readers, blurbs from authors, and any other information that may help our editors assess the content and early reception of your new book."

④ MAKE USE OF "NEW RELEASE" ALERTS

We know, we know. It's a little confusing, but this is a different alert, and it's free. As long as you've added your e-book on the platform within seven days of its release—and your e-book fits their criteria—BookBub will send out a new release alert to all your US followers. Even better, the email will include your buy links, so you could well get some sales from this. It doesn't take a genius to work out that the more followers you have, the more people get this email.

To qualify, your book needs to be over seventy pages if fiction or one hundred pages if nonfiction. BookBub will also consider other types of books, including cookbooks, box sets, and children's picture books.

⑤ USE CHIRP FOR AUDIOBOOK DEALS

Chirp (https://chirpbooks.com/home) is an audiobook platform available to US listeners. It offers some great deals on audiobooks, and it is powered by none other than BookBub. If you have an audiobook on Findaway, you can apply for a Chirp audiobook deal via your BookBub account. As of the time of writing, it's still free to apply for a Chirp deal, so what have you got to lose? It's still relatively early days for Chirp, so you may not get huge results from your promo like you could with a BookBub Featured Deal, but who doesn't like getting their books out there and reaching a new audience?

6 OPT FOR PREORDER ALERTS

BookBub's preorder alerts cost only two cents per follower. If you have thousands of followers, you might be concerned about the total cost, but this alert only goes to US followers who have chosen to receive alerts from you, so it could be less than you think. Even so, this alert could give you a real boost on release day. If you get a lot of preorders via this alert, you might even have a bestseller on your hands. No guarantees, of course, but it's most definitely worth trying.

7 SIGN UP FOR BOOKBUB ADS

BookBub ads show up at the bottom of the email when BookBub sends out its daily emails. This can get you great exposure and those all-important clicks and sales. As with Facebook ads, you set your budget and your target audience, so these ads can be specifically targeted to, for example, anyone who likes a particular author in your genre. David Gaughran has a post including insights from BookBub's own Carlyn Robertson, which may help. Visit https://davidgaughran.com/clever-book-marketing-authors-bookbub-ads.

8 USE RECOMMENDATIONS

Sorry guys, but this is another US-only feature. If you're in the US, you can write reviews and recommend books, which is a great way to market your own books too. If you recommend books in the same genre or genres as yours, not only can you build strong relationships with other authors (always a positive thing!), but you could attract the attention of readers who'll look at your books too. And nothing is stopping you from arranging recommendation swaps with other authors to give all of you a boost.

9 GET ICONS FOR YOUR WEBSITE

You definitely want people following you on BookBub as you'll get the all-important preorder notifications (US only) once you hit a thousand followers. Encourage this by adding the BookBub icon on your website, along with your social media icons. Get the icon, including the HTML to add it straight into your website code if you're the techie type, along with the instructions if you're not, at https://insights.bookbub.com/bookbub-follow-bookmark-buttons-for-authors-websites.

10 CHECK OUT THE BOOKBUB BLOG

Find the latest info on BookBub right from the horse's mouth, as they say. The platform's blog includes information about book marketing, the latest trends, new BookBub features, and more. It includes a section with book marketing advice (https://insights.bookbub.com/category/book-marketing-ideas), and another one jammed full of self-publishing tips (https://insights.bookbub.com/category/publishing-tips).

Still want to learn more? Check out other resources for authors on how to master BookBub, such as David Gaughran's BookBub Ads Expert: A Marketing Guide to Author Discovery, Monia Leonelle's Get Your Book Selling with Bookbub, and BookBub Mastery: An Indie Author Mastery Guide by Nick Thacker. ∎

Gill Fernley

STEVE HIGGS

Fast and Furiously Cozy

Steve Higgs is a man of contradictions—a tough ex-army man who writes about a bad-tempered, crime-solving police dog and a bored housewife turned sleuth. He's also known as the British author who wrote over sixty books in three years. He is funny, a family man, and yet hyper-focused. He puts some of his success down to having the luxury of a garden shed, or as he calls it, a "log cabin" at the bottom of his garden that allows him to lock the door and write all day. But how did he get to the point where he earns seven figures, far outstripping the income of his previous full-time career?

STARTING EARLY

Steve showed promise as a writer at the age of ten when he won a school competition in southeast England. He was invited to read his story on the local radio station, and as he put it, "It just kind of stuck with me."

His family offered very little support, however. When Steve turned seventeen, he joined the British Army as eight generations of Higgs had done before him. But the story bug never let go, not even during

Why does a tough ex-army officer write Cozy Mystery?

> He feeds five ongoing series with a new book every two to three weeks.

his twenty-five-year military career, which ended with his retirement as Capt. Higgs. Steve says, "There's a lot of downtime in the army. So I'd make up stories in my head but never find the time to write them down."

He soon worked a well-paid corporate job, but when he was too busy for his baby son for days at a time, he knew something had to give. During 2018, while employed full-time, he wrote six books, often during his lunchtime. In 2019, he doubled his output, quit his job on his son's fourth birthday, and began writing full-time.

During his army days, Steve got used to sleep deprivation. He says, "You don't need nearly as much sleep as you think you do." True to his words, he gets up at five o'clock and starts working shortly after, fueled by copious mugs of coffee.

He set himself a challenge to write thirty books in twelve months and only came up short by one book. "I failed," he says, half-jokingly. To date, he feeds five ongoing series with a new book every two to three weeks.

NOT YOUR TYPICAL COZY MYSTERY WRITER

Steve writes in two genres, Urban Fantasy and Cozy Mystery. His first book was an Urban Fantasy novel about a paranormal investigator who refuses to believe in the supernatural. Everything he writes is infused with humor and hilarity, which has earned him a loyal following across both genres.

Why does a tough ex-army officer write Cozy Mystery though? Interestingly, when Steve created his character Patricia Fisher, he had no idea he was writing in the genre. In fact, he didn't even know the term until it popped up in readers' reviews of his books. "I've never read a Cozy Mystery in my life to date," he admits.

Steve grew up watching series like *Murder She Wrote*, *Midsomer Murders*, and *Miss Marple*. In contrast, during his army career, he witnessed enough savagery that he didn't want it to spill into his writing. There is no blood spatter, no arterial spray, and no sex on the page. He only recently realized that that was his author brand. "I write fast-paced, adventurous mystery books with a humorous lilt," he says.

But how is he so prolific? How does a writer create a book a month? While writing his first few books, Steve was so unsure about spelling and punctuation that he kept a grammar book and a dictionary on his desk, which he consulted all the time. In his words, his early books are a little rough. But even today, he sends his first draft to his beta readers, and after making corrections, he publishes the book. For him, the story takes precedence over editing or revising.

Initially, he got some poor reviews due to typos, but because he writes so much, he managed to hone his skill as he published book after book after book. His readers love him, his novels sell like hotcakes, and his writing has gone from strength to strength.

THERE'S MORE TO WRITING THAN CREATING WORDS

Steve loves that instead of creating new content, he can repackage his original novels and earn extra money selling paperbacks. In fact, he's been doing this since

> Everything he writes is infused with humor and hilarity, which has earned him a loyal following.

his very first book because to him, books meant hard copies. He had no clue that people read novels in electronic format. So he hired somebody to make him a cover and uploaded it. But because the formatting wasn't done professionally, his 113,000-word door-stopper novel was so expensive, he didn't think he could charge any more than the printing cost. As a result, he made two cents per copy sold.

To this day, Steve has never formatted a single book. He creates a Word document and then asks an assistant to upload it to IngramSpark, using a free code issued by the Alliance of Independent Authors (ALLi.) (https://allianceindependentauthors.org)

WHERE DOES HE SEE SELF-PUBLISHING GOING?

True to his philosophy, Steve has no time for the latest publishing trends like Vella. "I keep telling people I don't know what I'm doing, and they laugh at me because they assume I've got all the secrets."

Which he insists he doesn't. Instead, he focuses on what comes naturally to him: "Writing fast-paced, fun adventure that just keeps building momentum to the explosive ending."

When pressed, he admits that he does have his own dreams about using Kickstarter or YouTube to produce a TV pilot and selling it to Netflix or using it himself. He thinks that indie authors could go into that space in the near future to produce their own web series.

But he also doesn't want to overstretch himself with yet another new subject to learn. "I don't want to run too fast because I'm enjoying doing what I'm doing," he says.

> "I keep telling people I don't know what I'm doing, and they laugh at me because they assume I've got all the secrets."

Are you our next Featured Author?

Tell us your story!

writelink.to/featured

> Most importantly, he can now spend time with his young children whenever he wants, and that, to him, is the most important change of all.

DOES HE CONSIDER HIMSELF SUCCESSFUL?

Steve's been remarkably open about his success, going from earning seventeen dollars in 2017 to five figures per month last year.

Readers recognize him on the street. A British TV channel has approached him about turning his Patricia Fisher novels into a television series. Even his family members have changed their tune after initially laughing at his dreams.

When asked what success means to him, Steve becomes pensive. "I never set out to make a lot of money. I never had that in my head." All he wanted was to supplant his existing wage to support his growing family and pay for little luxuries like an excursion to the zoo or brief trips abroad. Most importantly, he can now spend time with his young children whenever he wants, and that, to him, is the most important change of all.

DON'T QUIT

Steve's advice to new writers is simple. "Don't quit. I could have stopped a long time ago when my first book came out and I got rubbish reviews."

When he wrote every day and no money was coming in despite publishing five books, he could have stopped. Days passed with no page reads. It took another year for sales to pick up with the publication of his Patricia Fisher series. If he had quit then, he would have never gotten the chance to do what he loves—writing, spending time with his family, and living life the way he wants.

To learn more about Steve, go check out his website at https://stevehiggsbooks.com. ∎

Marion Hermannsen

PLANNING TRAVEL TO A CONFERENCE?

Use miles.

Explore ways to make the most of your award miles.

Writelink.to/unitedair

Is Your Book Multilingual?

CONSIDERATIONS FOR THE TRANSLATION QUESTION

As indie authors expand their businesses, they are pushing the boundaries into new languages. While this is a great path forward, full of exciting possibilities, some issues arise when you don't speak the language you want your books to be published in. We're covering finding your translation team and marketing in other articles this month, so in this article, we'll cover some issues you might want to be aware of as you consider if translation is the right fit for you right now.

Especially in the realm of translation, you must trust the people you're working with. Do your due diligence, and understand that in the best-case scenario, the relationship you develop with your translation team or company is cooperative, not adversarial. This should be a win-win-win for all involved and hopefully lead to a lengthening of the term because the partnership has been so successful.

I'm not a lawyer, and I don't even play one on TV, so this is not legal advice. But this article will just raise some questions for you to investigate further on your own as well as give you some solid resources to help you on your journey toward ticking the multilingual box on your author bucket list.

INTELLECTUAL PROPERTY RIGHTS

In most countries, you own the rights to your work when you create it. When you hire a translator, however, different countries have different laws regarding the rights of the translation. The original words are yours, but the translation may be the property of the translator.

THE SEARCH

Where do you find translators or foreign rights buyers? Frankfurt and London Book Fairs are great places to talk to agents, foreign rights buyers, and other team members on this journey. If you can't attend in person, both fairs have information about their vendors, so you can virtually shop and investigate potential partners no matter where you are.

Do your due diligence to make sure that the buyer is who they say that they are. Visit their website and Google translate it and see if they are proficient in what they are offering to do for you. If their website has nothing to do with the type of work you want, proceed with caution.

THE BUYERS

Foreign rights buyers are more likely to be interested in your book(s) if you can show marketability in your current market. A strong sales record will give you greater bargaining power, as a successful book in one locale is more likely to be a successful book in other locales. In contrast, if your book is not successful anywhere, you will not have a strong bargaining position.

THE NEGOTIATION

Everything in a contract is negotiable. If you're not comfortable with something, then propose an alternate solution. Again, this should be a win-win situation and should not totally favor either party. If the contract is all in your favor, you may be dealing with an inexperienced vendor, which could be a waste of your time. If the contract is completely in their favor, well, why would you sign it? You are negotiating toward a mutually beneficial end.

THE TERM

You'll want to specify the length of time you are agreeing to sell your rights to the translation. Judith Anderle stated in her presentation at last year's 20Books Vegas conference that she's found that translation terms are typically shorter than other types of rights contracts. A shorter term may allow you to switch to another company if you feel the current company is not the right fit for your books.

THE TERRITORY

This will describe where the translation will be sold. Are you allowing for all German-speaking areas or just Germany? Will your Spanish translation be available in Mexico? South and Central America? Spain? Ask the company you're working with where sales have been successful for your genre in this language.

THE FORMATS

Discuss what formats the translation will publish in. Or if you are simply hiring a translator and doing the rest yourself, consider what formats are the most successful in that language and the territories where you want to publish. This may differ from the formats that are popular in your native language.

THE STYLE

The words or characters of a language are not the only differences. The style of your book or the way you use humor or describe people and other matters may not directly translate word for word. Do you want a word-for-word translation, or do you want the general flow and feel of the book to be mirrored in this new work? Consider and discuss this with your translator. You may want or need to work closely with the translation team to ensure that the translation has the desired result.

THE TIMELINE

How long will the translation process take, and will the final product be available for purchase in that market? That will vary considerably, so discuss this with your team or the company who is considering purchasing the foreign rights to your book.

IT'S A DONE DEAL!

Your behavior after the contract is signed is important, according to Anderle.. Let's say you are supposed to be paid in thirty days, but you don't receive your payment and don't follow up with them to ask where it is on day thirty-one, or you wait a long time to check with them. This weakens your legal position regarding defending the rights you delineated in the contract. Keep detailed records and pay attention to the agreed-upon delivery dates and times.

Make sure that your contract is clear and covers all the issues applicable to your project we've discussed above and any others that arise in the months and years to come. Lawyers can be expensive, but especially in the realm of translations, ignorance or a lack of clarity may be more costly still.

As you consider and move toward what works best for you when it comes to multilingual publishing, we wish you well and would love to hear what's working for you.

For further information, check out *How Authors Sell Publishing Rights: Sell Your Book to Film, TV, Translation, and Other Rights Buyers* by Orna Ross and Helen Sedwick. At the time of writing, they are updating the book for more current information and will have it ready before the London Book Fair the first part of April, if not sooner. Be sure and browse their other guides as well—they are all excellent resources.

Judith Anderle's presentations at the 20Booksto50K® conference in Vegas November 2021 are also packed with great advice as she leads the team at LMBPN in selling their rights worldwide:

- Foreign Rights: https://www.youtube.com/watch?v=6YL1Mh9fVEc
- Business Contacts in the Self-Publishing World & Relationship Management : https://www.youtube.com/watch?v=-o0gq6uh5aA
- Translations Panel: https://www.youtube.com/watch?v=rdC4KY4L5X4

Joanna Penn at https://TheCreativePenn.com is very open about her experiences with translating her books into German as well as how she deals with the marketing question when she doesn't speak German.

The Self Publishing Show has covered translations on several of their podcasts. See https://selfpublishingformula.com/?s=translation. ∎

Alice Briggs

There's No "I" in Translate

WHAT'S IT TAKE TO FIND YOUR DREAM TRANSLATION TEAM?

Every author throughout history could likely recall a time they stared hopelessly at a blinking cursor or a pen hovering just above the page. And just as you know the importance of choosing the right words, you probably also know the struggle of finding them. Yet many times, only you, the author, seem to be able to identify the exact word you've been looking for.

So how do you trust someone to find that word for you when you aren't a native speaker of that language?

It's one of the many questions authors must answer for themselves when deciding to sell foreign translations of their work. Most major distributors support a variety of foreign languages—Barnes & Noble supports e-books in at least nineteen languages, and Kindle Direct Publishing (KDP) supports more than forty. And despite the grip traditional publishers have held on foreign markets in the past, translations are a growing revenue option for independent authors.

It's easy to understand why. Translations require little effort from the author to create. If done well, they make books accessible to a wider audience and create a secondary income from titles already on the shelf. But maximizing that

Translations are a growing revenue option for independent authors.

income requires finding the right languages—and the right people who speak them.

"A lot of people say, 'Well, you know, we're writing because we enjoy it.' I go, 'True, but you're publishing because you want to earn money,'" says author L.G. Castillo, who started publishing translations of her books in 2018. "I wanted to see: How can I increase my small part-time business? And one way was to do translations."

SPEAK YOUR READERS' LANGUAGE

As a Latina author, Castillo had already incorporated several characters who shared her culture into her books when she began pursuing translations, and she wanted to be able to share them with Spanish-speaking readers. Yet she was also willing to experiment, so when the first freelancer to connect with her offered an Italian translation instead, she jumped at the chance. She found a Spanish translator a short time later, and other opportunities in other languages have cropped up since then. As of the start of this year, Castillo had published translations of eleven of her books in at least one of four languages: Spanish, Italian, German, and Portuguese.

Author Bronwen Evans took a different route. When she first decided to explore the foreign translation market last year, she already knew the book she wanted to translate had sold well in Germany—as had books by many other

authors from New Zealand, where Evans lives. "The Germans tend to like the New Zealand authors for some reason," she says with a laugh. "I think they must like how we write."

But rather than using a translation platform, she reached out to a translator directly. "I didn't want my royalties, my copyright, owned by anybody else. And I didn't want to do split royalty," Evans says. "So I looked around, and that's where I found translators who would just do it for an upfront fee." The decision worked in her favor—although she had to wait around eighteen months for an opening in her translator's schedule, her first book made back her initial investment in a little over a month. Since then, she's published another German translation, and she's started work on a Spanish translation after finding an affordable translator through other authors in her genre.

Ultimately, when it comes to choosing which languages to pursue for translations, Castillo and Evans recommend researching the countries where your books or similar books in your genre have sold well. Speak to other authors about where they've had success or to your readers about their interest in certain language translations. Still, both authors say they've also made many decisions simply based on the opportunities they've found.

"Once you get the ball rolling, other opportunities can come your way. And that's why I've got to be a big advocate to take a dip in it [translations] as cheaply as possible," Castillo says. "Don't sweat the small stuff, you know? Just try it."

DO SOME DIGGING INTO YOUR PLATFORM AND YOUR PEOPLE

Of course, there's also the question of how to find the translators themselves. Castillo chose to upload her first books to Babelcube, a platform that connects independent authors with freelance translators, then marked them open for translation. The process was straightforward when it came to finding a translator, but after experiencing a months-long delay in publishing through the site and poor customer communication, she eventually transitioned to a similar platform, Tektime, by an Italian company, which she says was more responsive.

But Babelcube and Tektime have their limitations. Both distribute payments for authors and translators through a tiered royalty share—translators receive a larger percentage of a book's royalties to start, and that percentage slowly shifts in the author's favor as the book crosses specific revenue thresholds. Both platforms also retain exclusive distribution rights for translated works for the first five years, which means you won't get to decide where your book is sold until that time is up.

Babelcube

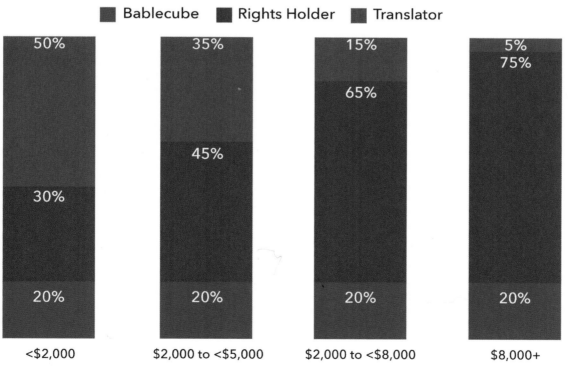

ROYALTY REVENUE SHARE BASED ON CUMULATIVE BOOK ROYALTIES (USD)

Bablecube ■ Rights Holder ■ Translator

	<$2,000	$2,000 to <$5,000	$2,000 to <$8,000	$8,000+
Translator	50%	35%	15%	5% / 75%
Rights Holder	30%	45%	65%	
Bablecube	20%	20%	20%	20%

Tektime

From	To	Author	Translator	Tektime
€ 0,00	€ 999,99	15%	75%	10%
€ 1.000	€ 1.999,99	30%	60%	10%
€ 2.000	€ 3.999,99	60%	30%	10%
€ 4.000	€ 7.999,99	70%	20%	10%
€ 8.000	€ . . .	80%	10%	10%

For some authors, including Castillo, it's a fair trade-off, especially when paying a translator up front isn't feasible. Independent translators charge ten cents per word on average for a translation from English, which means thousands of dollars invested at once.

But for Evans, the royalty share and distribution limits were part of the reason—though not the only ones—she opted to go a different route. She wanted to maintain complete control of her work, including the ability to distribute through Kindle Unlimited instead of a wide market. She also wanted to find a translator she trusted, which, for her, meant finding translators other authors in her genre had trusted in the past. "I've heard lots of horror stories, but I think it's because people haven't done their research," she says. "So for me, I always use someone who's been recommended or someone I know."

Castillo has faced similar dilemmas. But beyond wanting to ensure her translators would be accurate, she also wanted them to be able to fix "cultural components," she says, such as American expressions that wouldn't translate directly into another language. "I was fine with tweaking the story a little bit here and there to fit a different culture and their understanding of the essence of the story itself."

Her solution? Interview each potential translator and review their portfolios before deciding whether to hire them. Evans recommends a similar approach, and she also suggests reaching out to other authors about the translators they've used and how satisfied they were. And once you've received your chosen translator's work, find others who can review their finished translation. Evans opted to share her German translation with a family member who understands the language, and Castillo shared a few chapters of the translation with her readers who knew the language and had agreed to beta read the work.

As with almost every aspect of publishing, no single method is correct for creating and selling a translation. Whether you opt for a translation platform or independent translator, Kindle Unlimited or wide distribution, a language you'd planned for or just whichever opportunity you stumble across first, the strongest advice Castillo and Evans have is to do your research, figure out your goals for the translation, and have patience. "The big thing for me is don't rush it," Evans says. "To me, that's a lifetime investment that's going to be out there for a long time. So I didn't need for it to be paid off in five or six weeks. I would have been really happy if that had paid me back in a year."

"It's that mentality," Castillo says. "You know that saying, 'It's a marathon, not a sprint.' When we're talking 'marathon,' we're not talking months. We're talking years. I was in a years-long marathon, but I learned a lot." ■

Nicole Schroeder

Marketing Translations

Introducing your translated book to readers can be an excellent form of virtual travel. Just think of all those new friends you can visit when the world opens back up.

Travelers—especially writers—often collect surprising experiences and specific, colorful, and possibly useless details.

When your book travels, you may learn that Malaysia's currency is called a Ringgit (RM), that the Thema code for your genre is YGBH (children's interactive and activity: hidden object / search and discover), or that readers in another country have strong feelings about a vegetable featured in your book's title.

To market your book, you don't need to pass for a native. Show your interest in the rest of the world, use what you learn, and keep your slightly exotic flair. This is travel. It's okay not to know the correct answers. #NotFromHere Celebrate your small culture and language wins. They could be perfect social media posts.

With the pep talk out of the way, here are seven ways to explore the world of international book marketing.

1. "Get" Your Readers

Look for market research for the language and countries you are interested in so you can figure out what's important to the people you want your book to "meet." Open your mind to the world and let your book take you new places. Learn about international pricing with a free email course or watch basic videos on marketing in Germany.

2. Get a Publisher

Just because you're an indie author doesn't mean you have to do everything yourself. Consider selling foreign rights to a publisher for a specific time period. Or offer a short fiction piece to a magazine publisher who is willing to translate it for publication.

3. Get Categorical

You probably know how important browse categories are for your book on US retailers. Even more than keywords, which aren't used by all vendors, categories tell booksellers, librarians, and shoppers about the genre of your book.

When you dig deep into the metadata of your book, the international databases can help you find readers. If you have your own ISBNs, your ISBN agency (Bowker, Nielsen, etc.) allows additional information about your title in their database. IngramSpark, StreetLib, and GooglePlay Books allow international categories too.

4. Get Your Translator

Your translator could be the perfect person to help you with your foreign language author bio, book blurb, keywords, categories (sometimes the translation tools can't hack them), taglines, and hashtags. Think about marketing ingredients you can use repeatedly, such as that traveler's classic, "Where is the bathroom?" You might also ask your translator to point out a favorite quote from each chapter that you can pair with an image to use for advertising or social media.

5. Get Your Distributors

Look for marketing opportunities for your target country and language. Amazon has multiple marketplaces. PublishDrive has a different business model (monthly fee instead of percentage), but Chinese, Hungarian, Polish, Russian, or Romanian translations might make it worthwhile. Authors can apply for promotion slots as they become available. Draft2Digital has offered promotion slots with France's Vivlio. Kobo's team supports translations and original language books in France, Italy, Netherlands, and Canada. Germany's tolino media offers marketing support for authors who are direct with their platform.

6. Get Advertisers

Promotional services other than pay-per-click advertising are available in some other markets. Skye Mackinnon's book gives lucid and concise explanations of the sometimes overly complicated distributor and advertising options in Germany. Readers in the Know has an extensive list of promotion sites to check.

7. Get Connections

It's easier to meet people in a new place when you have a friend or a contact to introduce you. Share what you've learned about Malaysian Ringgits and team up for new adventures.

The classic marketing approaches of newsletter swaps, joint promotions, giveaways or even reader discussion groups can work for translations too. Find travel companions for you and your book in the Facebook groups to the right, and have a great trip! ■

Laurel Decher

RESOURCES

READERS

"What Readers Want" infographic and article: https://selfpublishingadvice.org/what-readers-want-2022

"How German Readers Find Books" (2017): https://indiesgogerman.com/how-german-readers-find-and-choose-ebooks-a-survey

International Publishers Association: https://internationalpublishers.org/our-industry-menu/statistics-and-market-insights

The New Publishing Standard": https://thenewpublishingstandard.com

"Tips For Translation, Self-Publishing, And Marketing In Foreign Languages With Nadine Mutas" The Creative Penn (paranormal author publishing in English, German, Italian, and French): https://thecreativepenn.com/2021/05/03/translation-and-marketing-in-foreign-languages

BOOKS

Self-Publishing in German: How to Translate, Publish and Market Your Books by Skye B. MacKinnon: www.amzn.com/B08TCJDCXH

Playing the Short Game: How to Market and Sell Short Fiction by Douglas Smith: https://books2read.com/b/bo6R14

How Authors Sell Publishing Rights: ALLi's Guide to Working with Publishers, Producers and Others: https://selfpublishingadvice.org/books/rights-licensing

Click on "preorder" to enter your email address to be notified when the book

becomes available. Free to Alliance of Independent Authors (Alli) members or purchase from the online shop. Read an excerpt on Jane Friedman's blog (updated in 2019): https://janefriedman.com/selling-books-internationally

CATEGORIES

DeepL translator: https://deepl.com/translator

Thema international book categories: https://editeur.org/151/thema

Helpful PDF for booksellers that gives examples of how publishers (like you) used Thema codes to describe their books: https://editeur.org/files/Thema/20200626%20Thema%20for%20Booksellers.pdf

BISAC codes: https://bisg.org/page/BISACEdition

GooglePlay Books list of accepted book category standards: https://support.google.com/books/partner/answer/3237055?hl=en

Amazon categories by marketplace: https://kdp.amazon.com/en_US/help/topic/G200652170

COURSES

Anja Bauermeister free German Marketing Mini Course (A solid overview from 2016): https://indiesgogerman.com/

"Pricing Books for an International Audience" by Zsofia Macho of PublishDrive (No longer new, but one of the best free Reedsy online courses.) https://blog.reedsy.com/learning/courses/distribution/pricing-books-international/

FACEBOOK GROUPS FOR MARKETING TRANSLATIONS

Marketing German Romance Books: https://facebook.com/groups/marketinggermanbooks by Skye B. Mackinnon

Author Support Network https://www.facebook.com/groups/AuthorSupportNetwork by Marie Force (The group covers many topics. Search for translations.)

The International Indie Author https://www.facebook.com/groups/441469159372773/ by Mark Williams.

PROMOTION SITES

Readers in the Know: 100+ Book Promotion Sites & Free Submission Tool (Click on the "International Coverage" column to see which countries are included.):

https://readersintheknow.com/list-of-book-promotion-sites German promo newsletters in Germany from July 2020. From *Die Self-Publisher Bibel* (For excellent directions and tips about these sites in English, see Skye B. Mackinnon's book above.): https://selfpublisher-bibel.de/marketing-tipp-wo-sie-auf-preisaktionen-aufmerksam-machen-koennen

RETAILERS

Overview and brief description of many international retailers and libraries: https://streetlib.com/distribution/retail-partners

Ask Kobo Anything: Going Global https://youtube.com/watch?v=JNeGYQqRO9c introduces contacts at Kobo Writing Life for France, Italy, Netherlands, and Canada. No German language contact because tolino media is Kobo's partner there.

Kobo Writing Life French Blog: https://kobowritinglife.fr

Kobo Writing Life Italian Blog: https://kobowritinglife.it

tolino media marketing contact available for authors direct with tolino: publishing@tolino.media Publishing directly with tolino requires a bank account with an International Bank Account Number (IBAN), but there's no requirement for the bank to be within Europe. Free advertising space in the tolino alliance network of stores is offered for e-books published to a professional standard, based on availability.

GETTING DEEP INTO TRANSLATIONS WITH DEEPL

There's nothing like a native speaker to translate a text. But what if advanced AI technology could help bring translated books into the world more quickly and with less of a dent to the author's budget? Would you be interested in that option? Honestly, who wouldn't be?

The question: Is translation software available to authors that rivals native speaker translations?

WHAT IS DEEPL?

According to its website, https://deepl.com, DeepL is "the world's most accurate and nuanced machine translation." Simply put, DeepL is a very user-friendly drop-and-click translation program. Once you've poked around on the main page, you might find a few user interface similarities between DeepL and Google Translate.

Exhibit A:

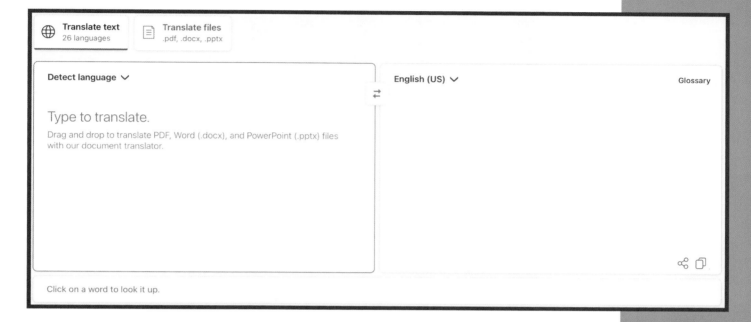

However, where DeepL really shines is with its available options and customizations. For example, if you select alternate wording, the surrounding text adjusts automatically. You can also translate snippets or entire documents of various file types, choose a formal or informal translation tone, create glossaries to customize how texts are translated, and use the built-in dictionary to better understand nuanced definitions.

The best part? There's a free version!

ARE YOU SURE IT'S FREE?

Yes, there is a free version, but DeepL has to keep the lights on, and they manage that task by offering various plans with additional features.
https://deepl.com/pro?cta=menu-plans

	DeepL Translator free	Starter $6.99 per user per month billed annually	Advanced $22.99 per user per month billed annually	Ultimate $45.99 per user per month billed annually
		Try for free	RECOMMENDED Try for free	Buy now
		Free for 30 days. Cancel anytime.	Free for 30 days. Cancel anytime.	
Maximum data security ⓘ		✓	✓	✓
Translate text ⓘ	Limited characters & volume	Unlimited *	Unlimited *	Unlimited *
Translate whole files (per user) ⓘ	Limited characters & editing ✓ Up to 5 MB file size	5 files/month ✓ Up to 10 MB file size	20 files/month ✓ Up to 10 MB file size	100 files/month ✓ Up to 10 MB file size
Formal/informal tone ⓘ		✓	✓	✓
Glossary (limited languages) ⓘ	1 glossary limited to 10 entries	1 glossary with 5,000 entries	2,000 glossaries with 5,000 entries	2,000 glossaries with 5,000 entries
Team administration ⓘ		For 2 or more users	For 2 or more users	For 2 or more users
Single sign-on (SSO) integration ⓘ			For 35 or more users	For 35 or more users
CAT tool integration ⓘ			✓	✓

* A fair usage policy applies

While the free version does have quite a bit of functionality, including limited characters in files up to five megabytes and one glossary limited to ten entries, certain features are only available with the upgraded plans. The starter level at $6.99 includes five files of up to ten megabytes per month, formal and informal tone, one glossary with five thousand entries, and up to two users for teams. At the advanced ($22.99) and ultimate ($45.99) levels, you get even more glossary, user, and file capabilities.

The option for multiple file translations per month might come in very handy when working with a backlist.

HOW DOES IT ACTUALLY WORK?

As a bit of a test, we enlisted the help of USA Today bestselling Romance author Lauren Smith. The goal is to see if DeepL can interpret period-specific language and get direct feedback from someone experienced with translations. First, let's plug in a short snippet from Lauren's regency romance book, *Seducing an Heiress on a Train: A Victorian Christmas Romance.*

When we flip the translation to see how it translates back, the text is quite close, with the context and intent of the phrasing mostly consistent, minus a bit of a change in the first sentence. To the untrained eye, the translation seems okay.

SO IT WORKS ON SOME LEVEL, BUT HOW DOES

IT COMPARE TO NATIVE TRANSLATIONS?

Our DeepL translation of the passage used above reads as follows:

> Rayne Egerton versuchte, die **aufsteigende Nervosität** zu unterdrücken, die in ihrem Bauch flatterte, als ihr Vater ihr aus der Kutsche half. Ihr Vater, Douglas Egerton, strahlte sie voller Stolz an. Sie versuchte, zurückzulächeln.

Fortunately for us, the author has already invested in a translator on this manuscript. Per the native German speaker, the translation of that same paragraph would be:

> Rayne Egerton versuchte, die **aufsteigenden Nerven** zu unterdrücken, die in ihrem Bauch flatterten, als ihr Vater ihr aus der Kutsche half. Ihr Vater Douglas Egerton strahlte sie voller Stolz an. Sie versuchte, zurückzulächeln.

The two translations do contain one discrepancy as highlighted. On the surface, this seems to be a fairly accurate translation, but what happens when we compare dialogue, which is often much more nuanced and may contain even more period-specific phrasing?

In examining larger blocks of text with complex structures, such as passages of dialogue, we see quite a few more discrepancies, and that is without considering punctuation differences

Here's the original passage of dialogue in English:

"It's my first English ball, Father. What if I don't know the right dances or say the wrong thing to one of the peers? The titles still confuse me." She had spent the last month reading a copy of *Debrett's Peerage* as she tried to understand the complicated system. Rayne still felt completely uncomfortable with all of the modes of address. At home, a woman was either a *Miss* or a *Mrs.*, and a man was simply a *Mr.* There were no earls, dukes, viscount, barons, or knights. Here it was all *Lord this* or *Right Honorable that*. And trying to keep their order of importance straight… It was all too much.

Here's the DeepL translation into German:

"Es ist mein erster englischer Ball, Vater. Was ist, wenn ich nicht die richtigen Tänze kenne oder das Falsche zu einem der Kollegen sage? Die Titel verwirren mich immer noch." Sie hatte den letzten Monat damit verbracht, eine Ausgabe von Debrett's Peerage zu lesen, um das komplizierte System zu verstehen. Rayne fühlte sich immer noch völlig unwohl bei all den Anredeformen. Zu Hause war eine Frau entweder eine Miss oder eine Mrs., und ein Mann war einfach ein Mr. Es gab keine Grafen, Herzöge, Vicomte, Barone oder Ritter. Hier hieß es nur Lord dies oder Right Honourable das. Und der Versuch, die Rangordnung einzuhalten… Das war zu viel.

And finally, the native German speaker's translation:

»Das ist mein erster englischer Ball, Vater. Was ist, wenn ich die richtigen Tänze nicht kenne oder einem der Herren das Falsche sage? Die Adelstitel verwirren mich immer noch.« Sie hatte den letzten Monat damit verbracht, eine Ausgabe von *Debretts Peerage* zu lesen, während sie versuchte, das komplizierte System zu verstehen. Rayne fühlte sich bei all den Anreden immer noch völlig unwohl. Zu Hause war eine Frau entweder eine *Miss* oder eine *Mrs.*, und ein Mann war einfach ein *Mister*. Es gab keine Grafen, Herzöge, Viscounts, Barone oder Ritter. Hier war alles *Lord dies* oder *Der Ehrwürdige das*. Und zu versuchen, sich die Reihenfolge ihrer Wichtigkeit zu merken … Es war alles zu viel.

and loss of formatting. But does this mean that DeepL isn't as good as the native speaker? Maybe.

To better understand how well the AI translation compares, we went straight to the source: the same German translator who worked on the above manuscript, Corinna Vexborg at The Novel Translator, https://thenoveltranslator.com.

"Generally speaking, translation softwares are a great tool to aid a translation," Vexborg writes, "in that it means the translator spends a lot less time looking up less familiar words. But an author should never, ever attempt to translate a novel by solely relying on software. It is a software, not a human being. It has a brain but no heart." She goes on to say that when the software is paired with a translator to avoid instances where the translations are "a bit dodgy" or outright wrong, it can be helpful to both parties.

Vexborg also provided a detailed explanation of the differences between the DeepL translation and her word choices, which showed that DeepL's AI struggled to understand language conventions, often with titles, and popular conversational or fluent usage. Word selections that would have helped the reader clarify the author's intent were partially lost in favor of literal translations that would read as very formal or awkward.

From an author's perspective, "DeepL seems to have a very decent translation from language to language when the wording you are using is straightforward," Smith writes. Smith concluded that she would likely use the software for very short sections of text or more formal pieces, such as an author bio, but would likely avoid using the program for anything longer, especially texts with pop culture references, historical language, or slang.

The verdict: The comparison shows us that DeepL is a great tool to have in your arsenal, but the skill and accuracy of a native translator has yet to be equaled.

Fret not! We don't have to worry about machines taking over just yet. For now, we'll let AI help with the small stuff and leave world domination for another day. ■

Bre Lockhart

Tech Tools

Courtesy of IndieAuthorTools.com
Got a tool you love and want to share with us?
Submit a tool at IndieAuthorTools.com

REEDSY TRANSLATORS

A listing of literary translators for hire. Get a quote and have your questions answered by pros.
https://reedsy.com/translation/book-translator

TOMEDES

High quality literary translation services by professional literary translators. Tomedes provides the best literary translation quotes. Get the best combination of low cost, high quality and fast delivery language translation services from Tomedes.
https://www.tomedes.com/literary-translation.php

BABELCUBE

Book Translation & Publishing | Authors & Freelance Translators Team Up
15+ languages
https://www.babelcube.com/

TranslationRights.com

TRANSLATION RIGHTS

A Free Translation Rights Marketplace for Print, Audio, and eBooks.
https://translationrights.com/

---

ulatus localize to globalize

ULATUS

At Ulatus, we only work with highly qualified translators. With over 3000+ handpicked translators we're also able to find you the best experts based on your budget and project requirements.
https://www.ulatus.com/

Head in the Clouds

AMAZON AWS BASICS FOR AUTHORS

In 1984, the first *Terminator* film thrilled audiences, and we were introduced to SKYNET, the network of supercomputers powering the world, described by one character as "hooked into everything, trusted to run it all … a new order of intelligence."

Back then, the concept of email was still somewhat fantastical, and the idea that homes would one day be smart and powered by voice commands seemed decades away. Of course, our colleagues writing Sci-Fi (and perhaps Post-Apocalyptic) might have suspected it, but the rest of us remained blissfully ignorant of what was just around the corner.

Fast forward to 2022. You may be tempted to think of Amazon as our conduit to book sales or a shopping portal, but that would overlook its reality: Amazon is a global cloud-computing network, powering many of the world's applications through what it calls Amazon Web Services, or AWS.

WHAT IS AWS?

What is AWS:
https://www.youtube.com/watch?v=a9_D53WsUs

According to its website, AWS is "the world's most comprehensive and broadly adopted cloud platform, offering over 200 fully featured services from data centers globally." Simply put, AWS is used by companies to build, test, and run cloud-based applications. These range from the very simple, such as basic file storage, to the complex, such as tracking and communicating with satellites.

Because AWS offers so many products, it's a near certainty that you're an end-user in one way or another. Netflix and other streaming services use their storage and content delivery solutions. Your voice-powered devices utilize their natural language recognition software to understand when you want to turn on a light or stream your Taylor Swift playlist.

Websites you visit could be hosted on an AWS Lightsail or EC2 server, protected by Amazon's Cloudfront firewall. Email might be routed through the Simple Email Service (SES). If you look at a map on your mobile device, you could be using the Amazon Location Service or their AWS Amplify service, and the map app was likely tested using an AWS Device Farm.

And certainly, anything you do is streamed into one of their data lakes and then shared, distributed, and analyzed in too many ways to count. Third-party companies have the option of paying to access your data. Does this sound like an invasion of privacy? It would be, had you not ticked the box agreeing to the terms of service that discloses that it's done when you signed up.

If you're getting SKYNET vibes, you're not alone. Ethicists and legislators around the world are grappling with how to manage the repercussions of this much information being controlled and run through one company. Cryptocurrency, blockchain, robotics, virtual reality, augmented reality, and quantum computing will soon become as common as email and websites, and AWS is on the forefront of the technology that powers them.

HOW AUTHORS CAN USE AWS

If you're intrigued rather than running to build an off-grid hut in the wilderness and start your doomsday prepping, there are some ways authors can leverage the benefits of AWS, chiefly the cost. Many products have a long free trial period, and after that you pay for only what you use. Often, the cost amounts to just pennies per month.

While there are more than two hundred AWS products, three have immediate and practical applications for indie authors: Amazon S3 Storage, Amazon Lightsail, and Amazon Polly.

Amazon S3 Storage

Think of Amazon S3 as an external hard drive. Rather than plugging it into your home computer, it's connected in the cloud and can store files of all types securely.

Pro tip: Back up your works in progress whenever you save or exit your document. It's also possible to archive and keep anything related to a project in a folder in the cloud called a "bucket" that can be encrypted to the highest possible levels, such as the Federal Information Processing Standard (FIPS) 140-2 used by the US and Canadian governments.

Chances are your manuscript doesn't need CIA code-word clearance, but it should comfort you to know that should you ever need to keep throngs of fans from trying to hack your computer to leak the contents to the world, they are safe and tucked away securely.

Amazon S3 also integrates with your WordPress website, and many plugins have easily configured plugins ready to deploy.

- Backup Guard Pro: Creates backup files, ensuring your website can be restored quickly if it's compromised. (Bonus Video: How to Set Up Your WordPress Website Backup)
- Download File Secure: Secures storage of your PDFs and EPUBs for distribution to paid customers or to ARC or beta readers.

Pro tip: Never share your files by uploading them to the WordPress Media folder. It's a known security hole that hackers use frequently to steal your files and upload them to piracy sites. They could also replace the file with malware. Better to use a program that secures and encrypts your download, such as Amazon S3 or a service like BookFunnel.

Amazon Lightsail

Website hosting can be confusing. On one end of the hosting spectrum are WordPress-dedicated services, such as Namecheap's EasyWP and Word-Press.com, both of which offer a stripped-down feature set and restricted design choices. They're cheap and easy to use, but you can quickly outgrow them.

On the other end of the hosting spectrum is what's known as shared hosting. This option is relatively inexpensive but bundles your site on a server with other websites. If one of your "neighbors" sends spam or hosts illegal content, you could become guilty by association and lose your Google ranking, or worse, be banned altogether.

Lightsail is a balance between the two, offering full, feature-rich WordPress hosting with one-click installation and also a dedicated IP address, so your digital reputation is yours alone to manage. If you have multiple sites, they offer dedicated servers starting at $3.50 per month.

Although Lightsail has some key advantages noted above, it's probably best for those with a moderate level of technical savvy. It does take some digging through documentation and videos to get started, but once you're up and running, it's a lightning-fast and secure option, powered by one of the world's largest and most connected internet companies.

Amazon Polly

Amazon Polly converts text to speech using neural, natural-sounding voices in multiple accents and dialects. Using the AWS interface in Polly, you can copy and paste up to five thousand characters of text and listen as it plays back what you typed in multiple voices. When you hear one you like, you can download the MP3. Use it to create marketing materials using snippets of alternating dialog in character voices to then create short social media ads or TikTok videos for promotion, for example.

Polly can also be used to read back a manuscript to listen for errors or convert larger text files to MP3 files. This isn't a built-in feature with Polly, but because AWS is merely the engine behind the scenes, it can be accomplished using a service like Zapier or Integromart, which are designed to build automations to connect apps.

Amazon also provides a WordPress plugin that converts blog posts to audio automatically.

Although Amazon AWS isn't self-aware yet, it's certainly the stuff of writer's dreams as to what it will be able to do in the future. For now, it's a powerful tool in an author's arsenal with limitless possibilities of what to do with it. ■

Chelle Honiker

To see an example of this plugin in action, look for the "Listen to this article" feature at the bottom of articles on the Indie Author Magazine website.

Podcasts We Love

AskALLi Podcast: Advanced Self-Publishing
Hosted by Orna Ross and Joanna Penn

Top tips and tools for running a successful author business, plus analysis of the latest self-publishing news and trends.

This show is for those who know how to self-publish and want to expand their income and influence.

https://selfpublishingadvice.org/podcast/

Novel Marketing
Author Media presents Novel Marketing the longest-running book marketing podcast in the world. This is the show for writers who want to build their platform, sell more books, and change the world with writing worth talking about.

Whether you self publish or are with a traditional house, this podcast will make book promotion fun and easy. Thomas Umstattd Jr. interviews, publishers, indie authors and bestselling traditional authors about how to get published and sell more books.

https://podcasts.apple.com/us/podcast/novel-marketing/id721122555

Entrepreneur Publishing Academy
Make no mistake; if you're an author, you're an entrepreneur. You're selling the world on your book, aren't you? Of course, it's not as easy as launching a business and then tossing any old book up on Amazon. That's why Entrepreneur Publishing Academy teaches entrepreneurs to publish books on the specific topic and in the specific way that will launch or grow their businesses.

https://www.legacylaunchpadpub.com/podcast

Emergency Medical Services

As authors, we put our characters through a variety of dangerous situations and often end up with some injured or ill. When we do this in a modern world, that character may encounter Emergency Medical Services (EMS) teams in their community. These highly trained medical professionals are seldom noticed by anyone until they're needed. Then they're a crucial part of a solution, cure, or trip to the hospital. Then the details matter.

HOW TO CALL AN AMBULANCE

Various emergency numbers around the world are used to contact emergency services. Take some time to research the one used in your story's setting. In the United States, Mexico, and Canada, you dial or text the numbers 911 to access police, fire, and EMS dispatchers. This is also true for many (but not all) South and Central American countries and for most islands in the Caribbean.

Most countries in Europe and all European Union countries use 112. In addition to 112, the United Kingdom still maintains the legacy 999 number. Many parts of the British Commonwealth around the world use 999 as well. Notable exceptions are Australia, which uses 000, and New Zealand, which uses 111. If you're not sure, do a quick internet search to nail down the correct number.

WHO SHOWS UP

First and foremost, don't call the first responders who show up in the ambulance "ambulance drivers." This is like calling an architect a "pencil pusher." Sure, it's sometimes a correct task description, but it's far from the only job done by the responding medical teams. In many parts of the world, including the US, UK, and Canada, you're safe calling the responders "paramedics," the most highly trained designation for field medical providers.

Some countries have medical doctors or registered nurses who respond with ambulances along with paramedics. Take some time to familiarize yourself with how the EMS system works in your character's location. You can usually do this by country, since many have centralized emergency services organizations.

The US doesn't have a single centralized model for ambulance services. Instead, a mishmash of different services provides emergency medical care. This includes fire department ambulances seen in many major East Coast cities and communities like New York, Philadelphia, and Baltimore. Others contract with private ambulance companies to provide care and transport in their jurisdictions. This is more common in communities on the West Coast, though the practice is spreading in other parts of the country. Lastly, a few communities even have ambulances run by police departments. The

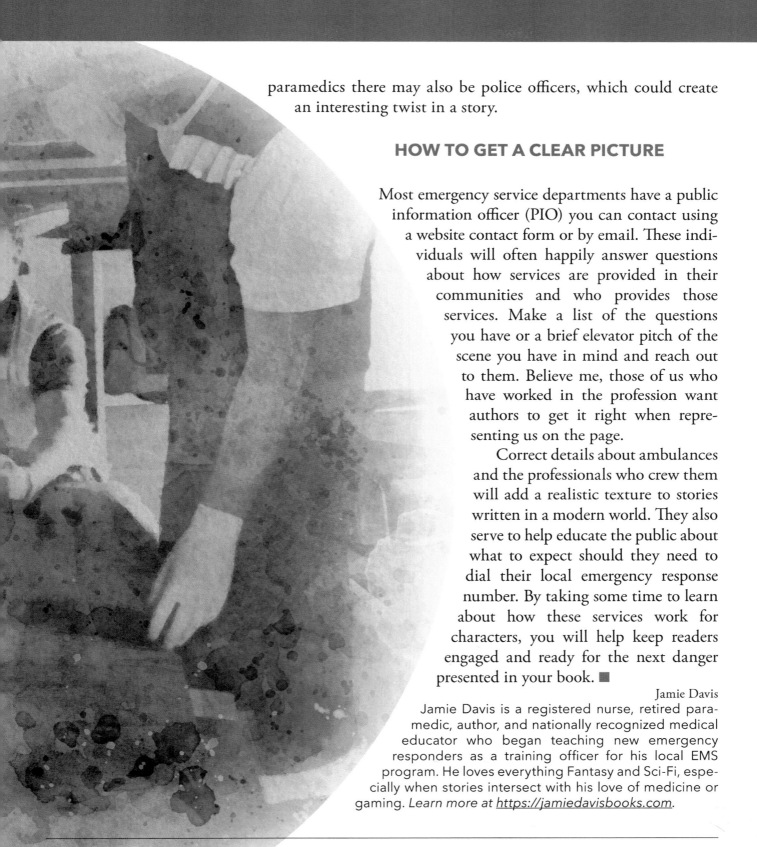

paramedics there may also be police officers, which could create an interesting twist in a story.

HOW TO GET A CLEAR PICTURE

Most emergency service departments have a public information officer (PIO) you can contact using a website contact form or by email. These individuals will often happily answer questions about how services are provided in their communities and who provides those services. Make a list of the questions you have or a brief elevator pitch of the scene you have in mind and reach out to them. Believe me, those of us who have worked in the profession want authors to get it right when representing us on the page.

Correct details about ambulances and the professionals who crew them will add a realistic texture to stories written in a modern world. They also serve to help educate the public about what to expect should they need to dial their local emergency response number. By taking some time to learn about how these services work for characters, you will help keep readers engaged and ready for the next danger presented in your book. ◾

Jamie Davis

Jamie Davis is a registered nurse, retired paramedic, author, and nationally recognized medical educator who began teaching new emergency responders as a training officer for his local EMS program. He loves everything Fantasy and Sci-Fi, especially when stories intersect with his love of medicine or gaming. *Learn more at* https://jamiedavisbooks.com.

MILITARY SCIENCE FICTION

Military Science Fiction infuses speculative technologies and interplanetary conflicts into the Military genre. The result is better guns, bigger battles, higher stakes, and a platform for social commentary. Science in Military SF tends toward the more realistic side, applying the same universal laws that govern tossed stones, cannonballs, and BFG projectiles alike.

This genre allows authors with a military background to apply their reality-based experiences, but civilians with a solid grounding in the genre's conventions can use Military SF to add conflict, strategy, and structure to personal journeys of friendship, rivalry, and leadership.

HISTORY OF THE FUTURE

Like most science fiction, Military SF extrapolates current experience into a speculative future. Speculation about martial conflict benefits from a solid understanding of how armed tactics have evolved through history, including aspects that have remained unchanged for thousands of years.

Writers need to consider the evolution of weapons and vehicles, but also revolutions in intelligence gathering, communications, supply-chain management, field medicine, and more.

MILITARY ORGANIZATIONS OF THE FUTURE

Characters in Military SF typically operate within military organizations. Given the vast distances between starships and their planet-side bases, analogous to ships at sea, tradition has borrowed from a naval influence with fleet admirals, ship captains, and on down the chain of command to overworked ensigns and fresh-faced cadets, often divided across functional commands and departments. Ship complements may include civilian technicians, consultants, family members, and workers, while many ships will also carry an obligatory complement of space marines and fighter-craft pilots.

Unlike in some other genres, where characters can freely wander off on spontaneous adventures, characters in Military SF have commanding officers, mission parameters, rules of engagement, and career aspirations. Structure and discipline are the rule. Going rogue is an exception that may come with serious consequences.

SOLDIERS OF THE FUTURE

Advanced technology may remove some limitations of human biology, but human psychology is harder to change. The title character in the *Murderbot Diaries* series by Martha Wells is a human-derived artificial construct designed to serve humans as a Security Unit. But upon overriding its governor module, Murderbot develops emotional attachments, desires, a love of soap operas, and other human quirks that make it a compelling protagonist.

The future soldiers of Military SF may be genetically enhanced or engineered, partially cybernetic, governed by neurochemical injec-

tions, or part alien. They may be a bunch of human engrams in a robot shell or 98 percent nanite by volume. But at their core, at least for the characters we're meant to care about, these characters should remain human.

ALIENS OF THE FUTURE

Many gripping stories have been told about humans fighting other humans in space or on alien worlds, but Military SF also makes use of aliens and AI combatants. Nonhumans can serve as enigmas, whether enemies, allies, or soldiers living and fighting alongside human soldiers in an integrated unit.

Nonhuman enemies offer up nonconventional tactics, new technologies, and biological quirks that require constant countermeasures. Nonhuman allies are often one clumsy cultural misunderstanding away from open hostility. And nonhuman soldiers within a platoon allow writers to explore what being human really means and how we're maybe not so different after all.

SOCIAL ISSUES OF THE FUTURE

Modern Military SF commonly traces its start back to Robert Heinlein's 1959 novel, *Starship Troopers*. Since then, the genre has developed alongside real-life militaries dealing with issues of racial integration, the role of women in combat, substance abuse, sexual abuse and harassment in the ranks, and the role of sexual orientation and gender identity in determining who gets to serve at all.

With the migration of human populations into a galaxy of alien cultures or with the arrival of technologically superior aliens on Earth, issues of colonialism will inevitably arise. Becoming conversant with current dialogues on this issue may help a Military SF author craft thoughtful and nuanced commentary without stumbling into uncomfortable or disrespectful territories. ∎

Greg R. Fishbone

MILITARY SF TROPES

1. *Powered Armor*: A wearable suit that enhances the strength, endurance, and sensory range of its wearer in addition to providing protection from harm. Jet boots optional.
2. *Mecha*: A battle vehicle controlled by one or more pilots that takes the form of a humanoid walking tank at least part of the time, especially common in anime- and manga-inspired works.
3. *Dropships*: These cramped personnel carriers transport troops through a turbulent journey from orbit directly into a planet-side battleground.
4. *BFGs*: Big F'n Guns. The warrior with a BFG becomes an army of one. The BFG-mounted ship becomes an armada.
5. *Clone Armies*: I'm not a number, I am a human being, and so are my thousands of identical twin brothers-in-arms. They call me the funny one.
6. *The Big Picture*: Frontline troops are expected to follow orders, often without knowing the ultimate objective of a military campaign. Will they still follow orders if they glimpse the bigger picture?
7. *Dial It Up to 11*: An over-the-top, extreme situation, weapon, or character trait. This overused trope should be used with care, or even better, avoided.
8. *Suicide Squad*: Some missions call for specialized skills of a criminal nature, an expendable crew of unwilling rogues, and the plausible deniability that comes with operating outside official channels.
9. *Going Rogue*: Whether sneaking behind a CO's back or staging a mutiny against the captain, there's no taking it back if things go sideways.
10. *Out of Retirement*: Just one final mission after the previous final mission, because you crave more of an adrenaline rush than you can get on that Montana horse farm.

Choosing the Right Chair

As writers, we can't avoid spending time sitting in a chair, and this can lead to both bad posture and pain. This pain is often, although not exclusively, in the back, neck, and shoulders. When it's time to think about a new work chair, you need to find one that meets all your needs.

BUDGET

For most of us, budget will be our first consideration, and like most things, the cost of an office chair varies widely. It pays to shop around for deals both online and off, as you can often pick up a practical chair for around eighty dollars. At the other end of the scale, a state-of-the-art chair could cost upwards of a thousand dollars.

SUPPORT

A chair with the needed support promotes correct posture. When typing or writing, your elbows should be at a 90-degree angle to your desk or table, and your knees should be at the same level as your hips, according to *Work Design Magazine*, whose article on workstation ergonomics includes several tips on how to set up your workstation to improve your health, wellness, and productivity. When you are sitting as far back in your chair as you can, it should also provide adequate lumbar support. A bolster cushion is a great alternative here if your budget becomes stretched.

COMFORT AND ADJUSTABILITY

The key to both correct support and comfort is adjustability. You'll be spending a lot of time in your chair, and you won't be able to produce your best work if you're uncomfortable.

Chairs can be adjusted to suit your needs in a number of ways. Height, seat, back, arms, and neck rests can all be raised and/or tilted, but apart from height, these do not come as standard features. Before you start looking, ask yourself what you need most.

If at all possible, do try before you buy—like a close friend, your chair will support both you and your writing. Some online companies allow returns for purchases that don't meet expectations, but do check the small print as you'll probably need the original packaging and be expected to cover the cost of the outbound freight.

And always remember: However great your chair, you still need to build in those all-important rest breaks. ∎

Jac Harmon

The Truth About Comparisonitis

PRACTICE GRATITUDE

Instead of comparing yourself with others, try comparing yourself with where you were a year ago. Focus on how far you've come, not how far you have to go, and you'll realize how successful *you* already are.

We've all been there. We've all done it. We've all compared ourselves with others. We look around and see the success of other authors, or we read a great book and feel as if we'd never be able to write that well. Thanks to social media and global connectivity, the success of others is more visible than ever before.

We are ultimately designed to understand ourselves, to reflect on who we are and where we fit into the world. Social psychologist Leon Festinger first explored this drive in 1954 and identified two main reasons why we compare ourselves with others: first, to reduce anxiety, and second, to learn how to define ourselves. He recognized that we can only define ourselves in relation to others.

Social comparison has its benefits as it helps us to keep our behavior in check, e.g., remembering our manners and knowing it's wrong to kill someone. It's in our DNA and traces back to a time when being part of a tribe and fitting in was the key to survival.

Usually, we have a bias toward comparing ourselves with people who are ahead of us, and because our brains are hardwired to have a negative bias, we focus on areas that we feel insecure about.

Social comparison can be a powerful motivator but can also undermine your self-esteem. If you're always looking at people further up the ladder and focusing on closing the gap between you and the next person, you risk becoming dissatisfied and never feeling quite good enough.

As we progress with our goals, the goalposts also tend to move. Therefore, we can easily forget how far we've already come. By learning to focus on what we've already achieved rather than on what others have, we can shift our mindset toward gratitude and find our own version of success. ◼

Angela Archer

HAUNTING FOR HIRE?

IF AND WHEN TO HIRE OR BECOME A GHOST ...WRITER, THAT IS.

Ghostwriters are a key part of the process for many authors. They provide a valuable service to help their clients produce books for various reasons. An older person who has lived an interesting life may hire a ghostwriter to interview them and compile their memoir for their friends and family to enjoy long after they're gone. Many famous people hire ghostwriters to write their books for them to provide their fans with additional information or a different perspective on their life and who they are. Popular speakers and ministers may hire ghostwriters to compile their speeches and talks into books that they can sell online and from the back of the room during events. Business people may hire people to do the same, using the book to establish their authority and as a referral tool.

Some people feel that this is dishonest or unethical, but in reality, a ghostwriter is another service provider who enables someone to publish a book they're proud of. In this way, they are not so different from a book cover designer or interior formatter. The author has purchased the words from the ghostwriter, and those words are now theirs.

When you receive the completed manuscript from the ghostwriter, this is typically a first draft unless negotiated and agreed upon otherwise. Ghostwriting is the writing part of the process, not the editing. Some ghosts are editors or may have a team that includes editing, but this will be an add-on expense and not included in the ghostwriting itself.

WHY HIRE OR BECOME A GHOSTWRITER

Most people hire ghostwriters because they have more money than time. They may also not have the skill to write well, and they would rather spend their time and effort on their areas of expertise instead of on developing a new skill. Although for many indie authors, this might not make sense, for business owners or famous people, especially, their time is much more productively spent elsewhere than on sitting down to write.

You might want to consider becoming a ghostwriter if you're a strong writer and enjoy working with others to tell their stories—either fiction or nonfiction. No, you can't add those titles to your portfolio, but you get a nice paycheck up front with no further marketing or selling to worry about.

We interviewed two ghostwriters, Lisa Thompson and Steve Bremner, who fill this niche for their clients. Many of their clients are speakers and business people who have content that they've produced, but they need help compiling that content into a book. They often interview their clients to pull out the information and ideas that the client wishes to include in the book.

LEVELS OF GHOSTWRITING

As with editing, there are various degrees of ghostwriting from compiling already written words into a cohesive manuscript to being given a topic and a word count and doing whatever research is necessary to complete the task.

FICTION AND NONFICTION

In Philippa Werner's talk at 20Books Vegas November 2021, she discussed ghostwriting for fiction. Her goal, when writing books under an author's name, is to so match the voice and style of writing that it is indistinguishable from the author's. She said that clients often hire her to write in a new genre so they can test the waters and see if it's worth their time in diverting their own time and energy.

Keeping a person's voice consistent in nonfiction is also important, as readers expect a book someone has authored to sound like them. Most often, the ghostwriter is using existing material for nonfiction, which may make this task easier.

When someone ghostwrites, they do not own the copyright for those words. The client owns the copyright. This is part of the reason that ghostwriters should—and do—command a high price. Once those words are bought and paid for, the ghost no longer has any rights to them.

In some cases, a ghost has been credited in a work, but this is not common. If you desire to be credited as a ghost or to credit a ghostwriter, discuss and agree upon the details in writing before work begins.

Ghostwriters are often asked to sign nondisclosure agreements before work begins as well. The limitations imposed should be agreed upon and stated clearly in this document. Not only may the client not want the ghost to share that they were involved in the project, but the ghost may also be privy to proprietary content and information that the client doesn't want disclosed. If you can't keep a secret, ghostwriting is probably not the right fit for you.

We recommend that if you have significant legal concerns, consult with a lawyer in your area who is well-versed in intellectual property rights.

ETHICS

Ghostwriting can include some gray areas. Philippa Werner states you should determine your ethical boundaries and not deviate from them, or ghostwriting will not be sustainable for you. These boundaries may include the topics or genres you're willing to write, the way you work with your client, and their access to you. This can mean turning down a large commission if you are uncomfortable with the topic or the ethics of the client. Ghostwriting is intense, and you can become very involved in another's world, so consider all the factors carefully before you choose to continue.

The type of work a ghost chooses and what a client agrees to also fall into this category. If you agree to certain conditions, such as length, number of revisions, hours of interviews or research, etc., then you both need to abide by that agreement. Compensate for significant overages or scope creep. If you hire a ghost to write a fifty-thousand-word book and you increase that to seventy-five- or one-hundred-thousand words, expect to renegotiate terms related to those additional words.

COSTS

As with so many matters in the publishing world, asking how much ghostwriting costs or will pay you is like asking how long a piece of string is. It depends on many of the factors we've discussed in this article. The length and the complexity of the project are both significant factors that can influence the cost.

Ghostwriters may be paid per word, per hour, or per project. Clarity on the length of the project is of critical importance, or you can expect to renegotiate if the project's scope increases. The complexity of the project, for example, and the time spent doing research or interviews may dictate the per-word rate, or these expenses may be itemized. We found rates from fifteen cents to four dollars per word, and Reedsy states that the average fee their ghostwriters charge for writing a book is around thirty-five cents per word.

Other considerations affecting costs include the number and depth of revisions, if travel is involved, what information the client can provide and its usefulness, and the schedule and deadlines. If you're in a hurry, you may pay a premium for a rush job.

The experience of the ghostwriter is also a significant consideration. A Pulitzer prize-winning author in their own right will command much higher prices than a beginner. As with any part of the publishing process, it's best to do your research and then find a ghostwriter or client that can work for your purposes and budget.

WHERE TO FIND ONE

Word of mouth is a great way to find a ghostwriter. Happy clients or those who know others who have had a positive experience with a ghostwriter make great referral sources. Some ghostwriters advertise, and places like Reedsy have lists of ghosts for hire.

Remember to look for a ghostwriter with experience in your genre or area and someone you feel you can work well with for the best results. A ghost who has written their own books is not necessarily the right fit, but they will have published works you can read and can discuss with you, which may be helpful. ■

Alice Briggs

With thanks to:
Lisa Thompson (http://writebyLisa.com) and
Steve Bremner (http://SteveBremner.com)

Books We Love

Courtesy of IndieAuthorTools.com
Got a book you love and want to share with us?
Submit a book at IndieAuthorTools.com

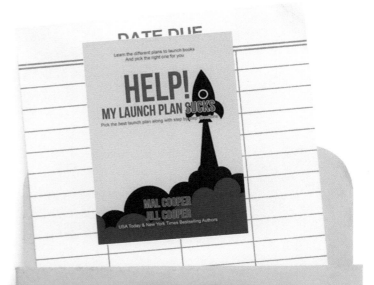

Self-Publishing in German: How to Translate, Publish and Market your Books

Learn how to go about translating your book, what to look out for when choosing a translator and what legal issues you have to consider. Decide how to publish your book as well as print and audio versions to give you maximum exposure.

This in-depth guide contains interviews with experts, insider tips from other authors as well as case studies that will help you succeed with your German self-publishing adventure.

https://www.amazon.com/Self-Publishing-German-Translate-Publish-Market-ebook/dp/B08TCJDCXH

Help! My Launch Plan Sucks

Find the best launch plan for your next book with step by step instructions!

Have you been struggling with how to launch a book or a series? Are you asking yourself an endless series of questions with no clear answers?

Mal and Jill will lay out multiple launch strategies, including pros and cons with KU, wide, preorders, and even services that exclude amazon entirely!

You'll get worksheets to plug your book and release date into, and then work backwards all the way to penning your first words!

https://www.amazon.com/Help-Launch-Plan-Sucks-Author-ebook/dp/B07YN75SWJ/

How Authors Sell Publishing Rights 2022 Update (pre-order)

Authors: want to know how to make more money from your books without writing another word?

Receiving self-publishing commissions or publisher royalties is only one revenue stream for your books. There are many other possibilities, from translations to video games, merchandising to print, but the rights world is a complex mix of formats, platforms, apps, territories and terms. Each market and each buyer offers different opportunities and operates by different rules. This guides shows you how to approach rights buyers, what they're looking for, and what to expect when discussing the license or 'sale of rights' for your book. You'll learn how to pitch, negotiate

and close a deal, and how to work with literary agents and global publishing companies. You will also be introduced to the Alliance of Independent Authors (ALLi)'s indie author rights program, which offers ongoing support.

Everything you need to begin successfully and selectively licensing your publishing rights for sale.

Note: This updated guide is expected to be released by the beginning of April.

https://selfpublishingadvice.org/books/rights-licensing/

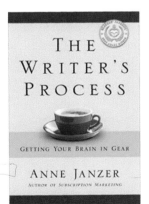

The Writer's Process: Getting Your Brain in Gear

The Writer's Process combines proven practices of successful authors with cognitive science research about how our minds work.

You'll learn:

• How to invite creativity and flow into your writing process

• Why separating writing into different steps makes you more productive

•How to overcome writer's block, negative feedback, and distractions

•How to make time for writing in a busy, interrupt-driven life

https://www.amazon.com/dp/B01G99B5LS/

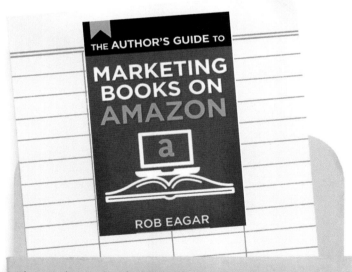

The Author's Guide to Marketing Books on Amazon: (2022 Update) (The Author's Guides Series Book 1)

This is the ultimate guide to selling more books at the world's largest retailer. Discover how to make your book stand out on Amazon's website and grab a reader's attention. Rob will show you how to: Increase sales, Identify categories, Secure influential customer reviews, Achieve maximum visibility with low-cost Amazon ads, Leverage marketing secrets within Author Central, Grow your author email list for free

The Amazon sales engine is waiting for you to use. Rob will show you how to tap into its full power, no matter if you self-publish or traditionally-publish, write fiction or non-fiction.

https://www.amazon.com/dp/B07K71DT3P/

AUTHOR·TECH·SUMMIT

May 18-20, 2022
AuthorTechSummit.com

INDIE AUTHOR NEWS & EVENTS

For the latest on news and events pertinent to the indie author community, please check out our interactive calendar here:

Got news or events to share with the Indie Author Community? Let us know at news@indieauthormagazine.com.

In This Issue

Executive Team

Chelle Honiker, Publisher

As the publisher of Indie Author Magazine, Chelle Honiker brings nearly three decades of startup, technology, training, and executive leadership experience to the role. She's a serial entrepreneur, founding and selling multiple successful companies including a training development company, travel agency, website design and hosting firm, a digital marketing consultancy, and a wedding planning firm. She's organized and curated multiple TEDx events and hired to assist other nonprofit organizations as a fractional executive, including The Travel Institute and The Freelance Association.

As a writer, speaker, and trainer she believes in the power of words and their ability to heal, inspire, incite, and motivate. Her greatest inspiration is her daughters, Kelsea and Cathryn, who tolerate her tendency to run away from home to play with her friends around the world for months at a time. It's said she could run a small country with just the contents of her backpack.

Alice Briggs, Creative Director

As the creative director of Indie Author Magazine, Alice Briggs utilizes her more than three decades of artistic exploration and expression, business startup adventures, and leadership skills. A serial entrepreneur, she has started several successful businesses. She brings her experience in creative direction, magazine layout and design, and graphic design in and outside of the indie author community to her role.

With a masters of science in Occupational Therapy, she has a broad skill set and uses it to assist others in achieving their desired goals. As a writer, teacher, healer, and artist, she loves to see people accomplish all they desire. She's excited to see how IAM will encourage many authors to succeed in whatever way they choose. She hopes to meet many of you in various places around the world once her passport is back in use.

Writers

Angela Archer

Having worked as a mental health nurse for many years, Angela combines her love of words with her love of human psychology to work as a copywriter in the UK. She independently published a novella and novel in 2020 and is currently fending off the lure of shiny new novel ideas to complete the second book in her sci-fi series.

When she's not tinkering with words, she's usually drinking tea, playing the saxophone (badly), or being mum and wife to her husband and two boys.

Laurel Decher

There might be no frigate like a book, but publishing can feel like a voyage on the H.M.S. Surprise. There's always a twist and there's never a moment to lose.

Laurel's mission is to help you make the most of today's opportunities. She's a strategic problem-solver, tool collector, and co-inventor of the "you never know" theory of publishing.

As an epidemiologist, she studied factors that help babies and toddlers thrive. Now she writes books for children ages nine to twelve about finding more magic in life. She's a member of the Society for Children's Book Writers and Illustrators (SCBWI), has various advanced degrees, and a tendency to smuggle vegetables into storylines.

Gill Fernley

Gill Fernley writes fiction in several genres under different pen names, but what all of them have in common is humour and romance, because she can't resist a happy ending or a good laugh. She's also a freelance content writer and has been running her own business since 2013. Before that, she was a technical author and documentation manager for an engineering company and can describe to you more than you'd ever wish to know about airflow and filtration in downflow booths. Still awake? Wow, that's a first! Anyway, that experience taught her how to explain complex things in straightforward language and she hopes it will come in handy for writing articles for IAM. Outside of writing, she's a cake decorator, expert shoe hoarder, and is fluent in English, dry humour and procrastibaking.

Greg R. Fishbone

Greg R. Fishbone is an author of science fiction and mythic fantasy for young readers including the Galaxy Games series of middle grade novels and the mythic fantasy serial, *Becoming Hercules*. Greg is the founder of Mythoversal, a project dedicated to broadening representation in classical tales by amplifying historically marginalized identities and restoring traditions erased by centuries of gatekeeping. As a former

Assistant Regional Advisor for the Society of Children's Book Writers and Illustrators, Greg co-directed regional conferences for authors and illustrators and presented workshops on a variety of craft and career development topics. He also served as president of the groundbreaking Class of 2k7 group of debut authors.

Jac Harmon

While studying for her doctorate in Medieval History Jac Harmon spent her time poking around in old buildings and reading manuscripts which gave her plenty of experience when it came to doing the research for her historical fiction. After many years spent working in university administration herding students she is now getting involved in voluntary work at a historic house and being trained in paper conservation. The idea behind this being that one day she'll be allowed to get her hands on some of the rare books in the library there. Not that this will help with her current novel which is set in the seedy criminal underworld of late-Victorian London. An era of gas lights and grime which was purposefully chosen to give her an excuse to indulge in her love of all things Gothic. Dark twists and bad weather are to be expected.

Marion Hermannsen

Marion is a bilingual author, working in both German and English. She holds a master of arts in English, Spanish, and Italian, as well as a diploma of marketing. She spent thirteen years both in London and Ireland while working in the finance and consulting industry.

Marion loves learning about writing craft and marketing best practices. She spends time mentoring other writers and enjoys the freedom of being able to work from anywhere.

She now lives in Frankfurt and is an active member of the local writing community, having published nine novels to date.

Her Irish husband has not only taught her the benefits of drinking copious amounts of black tea, but has impressed his Irish accent on her, to the amusement of her friends and colleagues.

Bre Lockhart

Armed with a degree in Communications and Public Relations, Bre Lockhart survived more than a decade in the corporate America trenches before jumping headfirst into writing urban fantasy and sci-fi, followed later by mystery under a second pen name. She's also one-third of a fiction editing team who probably enjoy their jobs a bit too much most days. As an experienced extrovert, Bre uses her questionable humor and red—sometimes other colors, too—glasses at writer conferences to draw unsuspecting introverts into her bubble of conversation; no one is safe. On her days off, you can find Bre camping and traveling with her family or organizing an expansive collection of lipstick at her home in Tulsa, Oklahoma.

Susan Odev

Susan has banked over three decades of work experience in the fields of personal and organizational development, being a freelance corporate trainer and consultant alongside holding down "real" jobs for over twenty-five years. Specializing in entrepreneurial mindsets, she has written several non-fiction business books, once gaining a coveted Amazon #1 best seller tag in business and entrepreneurship, an accolade she now strives to emulate with her fiction.

Currently working on her fifth novel, under a top secret pen name, the craft and marketing aspects of being a successful indie author equally fascinate and terrify her.

A lover of history with a criminal record collection, Susan lives in a retro orange and avocado world. Once described by a colleague as being an "onion," Susan has many layers, as have ogres (according to Shrek). She would like to think this makes her cool, her teenage children just think she's embarrassing.

Nicole Schroeder

Nicole is a storyteller at heart. A journalist, author, and editor from Columbia, Missouri, she delights in any opportunity to shape her own stories or help others do the same. Graduating with a bachelor's degree from the Missouri School of Journalism and minors in English and Spanish, she's worked as a copyeditor for a small-town newspaper and as an editor for a local arts and culture magazine. Her creative writing has been published in national literary magazines, and she's helped edit numerous fiction and nonfiction books, including a Holocaust survivor's memoir, alongside international independent publishers. When she's not at her writing desk, Nicole is usually in the saddle, cuddling her guinea pigs, or spending time with family. She loves any excuse to talk about Marvel movies and considers National Novel Writing Month its own holiday.

Ready to level up your indie author career?

Trick question. Of course you are.

*INDIE ^Author Tools

Get Your Friday Five Newsletter and find your next favorite tool here.

https://writelink.to/iat

Join the Facebook group here.

https://writelink.to/iatfb

COME VISIT
the *Cake Machine* STAY for the *Conference.*

Las Vegas
Nevada
November
14-18, 2022

writelink.to/20Books

20 BOOKS TO 50K®
A RISING TIDE LIFTS ALL BOATS

Printed in Great Britain
by Amazon

77841575R10047